Musings of Maria

Joelene Carlson

Presentation by *BookLeaf Publishing*

Web: www.bookleafpub.com

E-mail: info@bookleafpub.com

ISBN: 9789357212748

First edition 2023

To Maria,

*My first born. Who taught me to truly love and
to love myself.*

Our Maria

You know I dreamed about you,
For so many years before I met you.
The little girl who changed our life,
More than we could tell you.

I never dreamed of what you would look like,
When you were born, I knew it was you.
Your face was so familiar to me,
Like I had known you before.

I remember you staring at me,
From your daddies arms.
You were so tired but wouldn't sleep,
It was getting so very hard.

For 10 weeks straight we took it in turns,
Walking and rocking, 4 hours at a time,
There was nothing worse than the shake of the
shoulder,
Knowing the shift was mine.

Then one day you did it,
You knew your daddy was unwell,
You finally let us lay you down,
And mummy had a spell.

You are the smartest girl I've ever met,
You are so intuitive and wise,
We must have done something right,
For you to pick us and change our lives.

Like a lightning bolt you made your mark,
You stole our bed, our arms, our heart,
You came in fast and hard and strong,
Like a jolt right from the start.

Your sparkling eyes, your big bald head,
The way you laugh, the way you grin.
You are trouble times a thousand,
But I'd do it all again.

It's been one hell of a year my baby,
My mini me, my sweetest pea,
I never knew I could love like this,
The little girl who calls me Mummy.

Happy birthday to our Maria.

Haiku for you

Daylight and dawning
Endless feeds, but it won't last
You and me baby

Tiptoe

I tiptoe in
It's late at night
I look upon your face
Your eyelashes
Your soft pale cheeks
So peaceful now than day

I reach right in
Can't stop my hand
I stroke your soft brown hair
Your eyes they flutter
You toss your head
Your hands they reach for air

I didn't want to wake you up
Oh please just stay asleep
I tiptoe out, but look back in
You're smiling as you sleep
I hope you know that it was me
Missing my baby

Why you crying

Why you crying mummy
My hand it strokes your cheek
My fingers touch the wet spot
Where your tear has left a streak

Why you crying mummy
Cause I grew in such a rush?
Is that why you stay up at night
Thinking all too much

Why you crying mummy
You know I love you so
There's so many things I want to say
Things I just want you to know

Why you crying mummy
I will sit here in your lap
I will play with your t shirt
I will lay down for a nap

A little nap

Belly to my belly
Cheek against my breast
Sleepy milk dribbles down your chin
The baby has a rest
And instead of rushing
I stay there in the chair
I gaze upon your tiny nose
I stroke your golden hair
It feels so very long ago
You were tiny in my lap
You hated to be left alone
I rocked through every nap
Now you'd rather chase the dogs
Instead of sitting there upright
But I know you'll look for me
As you settle down at night
So sleep now little baby
Lay your head against my arm
And I will sit and watch you
I'll never go too far

SAHM

This monotony might kill me
I said but make it funny
You don't want your friends to know
You're just no good at mumming

You don't bake, you can't cook
You are too tired to clean
And in the depths of motherhood
You forgot you are Joelene

The girl in you, now pushed so low
She shouts to get let out
You make the bed, you change a nappy
You push those bad thoughts out

Each and everyday you struggle
You miss who you used to be
Your friends told you how blessed you are
To stay home with baby

Growing

Twelve months have flown by
But I lived through every day
And now you are one

Slow down mumma

Slow down mumma
I know you have work to do
I don't want you to leave
I just want to be with you
Slow down mumma
Can't the folding wait
I'm sorry that I fell asleep
I don't want to make you late
Slow down mumma
I know you want to weep
I'm not finished playing
But you say it's time for sleep
Slow down mumma
The dishes piling up
I promise I'll let you do them
When I'm ready to get up

Ten little fingers

Ten little fingers
Ten tiny toes
The sweetest long eyelashes
The cutest little nose
The crease in your forearm
The dimples in the cheeks
The sparkle of your eyes
The tapping of your feet
The smile that you give me
The crinkle of your nose
The furrow between your eyebrow
My darling sweet rose

I don't recognise the girl in the mirror

Her big dark eyes are wide and tired
Her skin is pale and soft
She's frightened and feels lonely
She's worried about so much

I don't recognise
This girl who changed so much
She went in just a girl
And she came out a full mum

Somewhere deep inside
Is that girl she used to be
But now she's someone different
She's somebody's mummy

My Sweet Girl

Back and forward
Forward and back
We rock and we rock
We pat and we pat
Your sweet little eyelids
They flutter and fight
But mummy wins this one
My sweet girl, good night

Memories

I took so many photos
Too many videos to count
I knew it would go so quickly
I didn't want you to miss out
I wish I could remember
All the little things there were
Because time has gone so quickly
And so many things are blurred

I remember how you scrunch your nose
I remember your sweet laugh
I remember the first time your crawled
I remember your first bath
I've forgotten when you first said dad
I've forgotten your first smile
I've forgotten so many little things
It makes me want to cry

But I guess it's not important
All the things I don't remember
We gave you all the time we could
Since you arrived back in December
And now I think about it more
As your birthday quickly nears
And in my heart I know
We did all for you this year

A long day

The sun has settled now
But you are just so restless
Another long day

Temperature rising

My back aches
My hands are numb
My toes are cold
Stuck on my bum
Your body tenses
It's hot to touch
You won't let go
You want your mum
I'll stay here baby
I won't leave you
Although I hurt
I'll stick it through

Just wait

Just wait until she's crawling
They say like I can stop it
And then you'll just be worrying
Of what she will hit

Just wait until she's walking
They say like I don't know
And then you'll be complaining
Because she'll be on the go

Just wait until she's talking
They say like it's a choice
As if I can stop her
When she's found her pretty voice

Just wait until she's running
Like I'm going to hold her down
This girl has so much freedom
I just will not keep her down

And while so much scares me
So much makes me worry
About this brave and wild girl
Who keeps my heart a flurry

Wild & Free

Thinking of a year ago
Of the day that you arrived
Of the shock and elation that i felt
When I looked down in your eyes

And now a year later
I've been blessed to watch you grow
To watch you become this girl I see
This girl I'm blessed to know

She sparkles with mischievous
She doesn't speak, she'll yell
She commands the attention in the room
I know I'm in for hell

I nursed you every temperature
To sleep every night
I won't forget the time I've spent
Blessed and at your side

I'll hold your hand through everything
I know you'll be just fine
My spirited girl, so wild and free
I can't wait to see you shine

Big strong girl

Your fingers once so tiny
Now hold my hand so tight
Your hair so dark the day you were born
Now it is blonde and light
Your eyes they change every day
But still sparkly and bright
You're everything I dreamed of
I hoped for with all might
And now I'm blessed to hold you
As you go to sleep each night

One

Happy birthday girl
Your first big day has arrived
Our baby is one!